Printed in the United States of America

For more information, address: ebonysandprincess@gmail.com

Black Minds Publishing is a national publications platform centered around the personal and professional growth of artists and creatives of the Black diaspora. At Black Minds Publishing we aim to give more visibility to raw artistic works, both literary and visual, that center on the healing process of the Black mind, body and spirit. We aren't concerned with the rigid expectations of academia or the "supposed to's" of artistic gatekeepers and instead choose to prioritize genuine works that have meaningful impact for its readers.

Names: Noah Humphrey/Knowa Know & Meryl Humphrey

Title: My Dream Carried Love

Description: Philadelphia, PA: Black Minds Publishing [2022]

Identifiers: 978-1-7375490-4-8

Many times in life we find friendships in the most unique ways. I became friends with Christina Barlow, the mother of Angela Jeana Ann Barlow, and Keisha Edwards, the mother of Shantee Nakhid Sayles through the most tragic of circumstances. Both young ladies lost their lives violently at the hands of monsters. The world can be such a mean and cruel place. These young ladies were beautiful inside and out and I never want the world to forget them. Christina and Keisha, I love you both dearly, and please know that I think of you both daily. I pray you are kept well and in peace beyond all understanding until you meet your daughters once again.

Meryl Humphrey

Table of Contents

Land Acknowledgement

As a settler of the sovereign nation, I would like to begin by acknowledging that the ʻāina(land) of Oʻahu is a part of the larger Pae ʻāina(group of lands) recognized by Kānaka ʻōiwi- the term Native Hawaiians use to refer to themselves as the bone holders of Hawaiʻi. I will use kānaka ʻōiwi as the term to honor their independence; connection to the bones of their ancestral grandmother, Papahānaumoku; and differentiation from Native American tribes/ colonized v. occupied peoples. We as a family recognize that her majesty Queen Liliʻuokalani yielded the Hawaiian Kingdom and these territories under duress and protest to the United States to avoid the bloodshed of her people. I, Noah Humphrey further recognize that Hawaiʻi remains an illegally occupied state of America and have engaged in community work and research to establish further ties to those I come across on the continent through my academic studies.

My family and I recognize that each moment we are in Hawaiʻi she nourishes and gifts us with the opportunity to breathe her air, eat from her soils, drink from her waters, bathe in her sun, swim in her oceans, be kissed by her rains, and be embraced by her winds. We further recognize that generations of Kānaka ʻōiwi and their knowledge systems shaped Hawaiʻi in sustainable ways that allow us to enjoy these gifts today. For this we are grateful and as settlers, we seek to support the varied strategies that the Kānaka ʻōiwi peoples are using to protect their land and their communities. We commit to dedicating time and resources to working in solidarity with all the Kānaka ʻōiwi along with those of Pacific Islander descent more specifically the Federal States of Micronesia and the lands that resided in that nation. Mahalo to Noel Kaleikalaunu Shaw for their dedication and care in reviewing this so that we can avoid dishonoring or discrediting those who were there before us and the proud descendants of Hawaiʻi. For further information, please read *A Nation Rising: Hawaiian Movements for Life, Land, and Sovereignty* by Noelani Goodyear-Kaʻopua, *From a native daughter* by Haunani-Kay Trask; and more Kanaka ʻōiwi authored books that express the history of Hawaiʻi and their reflections of honoring the ʻāina. May the Kānaka ʻōiwi reside in Hawaiʻi, the sovereign kingdom, till the end of time.

Preface

Grass Wasn't Cut With A Sickle

Since birth, I was cut from different grass
Doctors kept saying I was sick, that the trait was alive
But I felt that the grass was much more apparent
The garden around me was brown
But it was supposed to be green, flourishing
And at the age of 7, the lucky number at the Sinai Hospital
Where they could get to the root of the problem
A foreign doctor found a Thalassemia trait interacting with a Sickle Cell Trait
That's where Sickle Cell Thalassemia began
My garden was not cut from the rampage of health
Rather than the myriad of doctors producing their exclusion
My black panther parents roamed their origin roots
Their foreign sickle cell was found right after their birth
The Weed was emerging with the Mediterranean, so overseas where the ancestors walked
Overseas where my parents resided their bloodline and fight against systematic oppression
And even with their sense of the jungle, the variation of the weed Thalassemia existed.
Thus the Mediterranean bared fruit to the biracial sickle of Greece
The Panther engaged and enraged by the inner works of the foreign plant
That Greek ancestry in my father's eyes, they have caused pain in his child's bloodline.

Black Body Baptism

It was bigger faster and stronger in the Black Panther alliance
The tool of the brain cannot bring ill will even an illness
I couldn't fly or prowl like the panthers
But in my mind, I served as an HQ
I have developed my own writing style
The writing was my jungle
The prowl was in literary words and the world expanded
My vivid imagination from the lack of vivid blood flow
A way with words and accolades led me to debates
And the problems that were unresolved, I had a greater home
The neighborhood had me as their juror
I was a master of words and a good fighter in a battle of systemic problems in my area
And the blocks revered me as if I was a commander of the pen
The lieutenant of literature, a commissary of the common speech
Education through my teams emerged me in the baptism of the higher arts
I was trying to become the strongest learner and the student that challenges the white teachers
A Black Panther will not back down from a white teacher besmirching black students
Thus I was a commander in their literary freedom, the reign I imposed set a standard
Though there were cheers for me, I told them to look at the ones behind me more closely
There was a child that was greater than me, a scholar faster than my success in their cowls
Don't tuck your pocketbooks, your smiles, and the disgust you turned around
Those were the same boys that could've changed your future and the lack of eye contact
The tool of my brain was sharpened as there is a mutual work with all learning to combat the evil commanders that took our tools away
They will not deny my baptism into higher education, nor the black bodies that they told to stay stagnant in arrogant change. My alliance with the black boys in the classroom became their saving grace.

Part 1: Dreams Prepared

Until the Wheels Fall Over

(Inspired by the documentary "Pain Raised Me" by Heather Friese Banet)

If I had a message for the passengers like me on this journey
I want mothers with chronic illnesses to hear this: I would like you to trust your kids
The job called life, transportation and survival creates proportionally faulty engines in our minds
For me, my body, like my blood pressure, may or may not affect my bus trip there
I spent every week on a bus from LA to Fresno for 3-hour IV treatments
Twice a treatment, double the cost, half the education, and where is my rest week?
I tried to get doctors to understand, but they did not give me a rest stop for this journey
It can be the bane of my day or the glory that God gives to me during those hours
Gaslighted by the problems of undiagnosed doctors unable to craft or describe my body
I look at the veins in my hands from the repeated sessions and their false doctrine
I look at the children that I hold and leave them with my husband
I get up at 3 am in the morning for a 9 am appointment for half the medicine I've been prescribed
Because the wheels on the bus of life are not optimal standards
I can remember when I lived in Fresno California the sacrifices of my bus ride back for those events Carrying deranged ladies I fought because of their rudeness
Each week was the same routine, the same pain, to drag a 6-hour bus ride to the hospita

The visitors I had on the bus with me was the same way
The homeless looking for a ride and some change
The prisoners with their clear bags and lack of essential supplies haphazardly collected
Then just like bus passengers on the Greyhound, what fare would they pay for this heal-ing?
This chronic is not the tonic that loses the elixir of life away
And then if I moved, I would rather take a bus than hurt my family,
And then I pack my bags and my arm away
Finding a vein then getting a bus ticket home either strapped to an IV or on my bed in LA
And again, and again
The IV becomes corrosive to the sound of the world that does not hear my cries
Whereas a treatment left me more tired than those 3 am wakeups
and that when I woke up at that supposed time
If the only message I have for the lifelong journey in the medicine existed in a line
It would say

I did all I could DO
to NOT fall back
into a bed
and do it again

Aloha to My Happy Place?

Our move to Hawaii was a brilliant radiance of light
We visited the sovereign lands and from that move, the love of the land shone
That light, or love, made it our happy place
We bid our goodbyes to LA as we moved to Hawaii
We crafted and gave a brand of plans that would be a blueprint to our joy
For us, the move with the medical complications created a place of darkness
My condition is rare and being on an island that's 3% African American, our dream
was fading
So the treatment of the condition on this sacred land was an arduous task
Yet we moved forward and by the luck and power of God
Embedded in amicable prayer

We moved despite the fears of my condition, we found a Japanese physician
He would be the warrior of my blood, the person who would amplify my securities
With this doctor, I would have a happy place without sacrificing the joy of my
children or husband
My LA physician was well-rested and assured about the blessings on the land
And with this, the light similar to the rainbows chased across the state of Hawaii
Amidst rain clouds and sky shattering rain in ample multitudes of blue inspiration
Our reality was now with our family and with those 18 short months of planning
We found a happy place and a place to give my own healing a shot at happiness
I finally said mahalo to my sad predetermined destinations and aloha to my happy
place.

Aloha means hello in Native Hawaiian. Alo means presence and ha means breath therefore the
presenting being is breathing. This states that we are entering one's space and being respectful.
It is not supposed to be profited, only gifted in times of love and inner being.

The Prophet Unchained

We called for the rain in the circumstances unknown
We waited for the fruit to be flown in the Memorial Day blues
The rain itself was heavy and hectic with the work of the vets themselves
Prophetic veterans stomping in their boots
And I was stomping too in my misery
With my belly working out
And that I shouted with my voice to proclaim that that prophet would be born
That memorial day I sought the wine blessed by the high priest
And as I waited for the throne room the work of a modern bedchamber
My intentions became now a flush of open water,
My husband was surprised at the unexpected arrival of flooding
But no one thought he was supposed to be apart of this world at this time
And the prophet did not come out until 23 hours after the water broke
The stubborn child proclaimed against the assault of the doctors and nurses
With the C section in a defiance action
His first act was a prophetic cry to stay in and stay out of his own birth
His fastness and steadfastness succeeded our wild wishes
He talked before, walked before, and exceeded other children
His pearly whites were engraved in his gums before he was introduced to solid foods
The blessings to be able to chew before chewing
His eyes studied like a madman on the moves of those around him, specifically the
adults
And animals called his name as if he was in the Garden of Eden
His first complete sentence was "I am Tiger Woods"
Fitting for this monstrous prophet with growth unordinary
His milestones were reached before peers near 3 years older than him
The lantern that was his brain shone greater in his reading and walking
with his latter being second, no one could chain him and his strokes of genius
And with that, the barriers of the world could only hold him for so long.

The 2nd Coming of Noah

Likewise to the Prophet, there was another chance of rain
A 2nd prophet that lead forward after the one on Memorial Day
For 17 days and then on the 18th day it rained like a tornado sucking up water
Then "Noah" was born
8 days it continued to rain
The entire time I remained in the hospital
With the eyes of pregnancy and Sickle Cell
I watered the grass of my soul looking out the window
Seeing the visitors with raincoats, umbrellas, rain boots, and soggy bags
Moist phones, my requested food, foggy eyes,
The baby that was going to be born was going to be special
Never before had there been that much rain for so long in that region
The prophet brought rain and stubbornness but as I consumed television
I knew that the special works were seeing,
Lines of "you are not the father", "you are the father"
Maury was a prime example of my mindful exercises with a baby along the way
He waddled within my womb and heard this banter in the cascading rain brilliant with tears
These tears streaked the sky and the minds of the nurses caring for my hope
The calendar around me was nonexistent but the schedule for the nurses was my clock
These rotations made me aware of my time, the day, and other sections of my soul

Match Day

I have accepted the call to become a nurse to the brokenhearted
And you listen to my advice as if I were the head doctor
The neurosurgeon to your bitter demands
The doctors call me doctor, but I call myself too green for this work
The seasoning of the visits from those who are shipwrecked from bad relationships
Unhoused from situations that have caused them to doubt or worship love
It becomes harmful to the body but as a matter of fact, my own heart can't keep guessing
The symptoms that these patients keep getting out of their wits for
Is it the new drug on the street called Meryl's advice?
Am I really up for the task, that is the match made in heaven?

These people come right back to me like IVs empty from the usage of dehydrated customers
Patients see me on the last ends of their youth like Jesus
Yet rise into my eyes and say "Where art thou father" to my expertise
I want to get you healthy, I want to make sure you know the side effects
Don't seek those users, the free riders, the emotions, people wanting you for your body
I see the future pains and they cannot wrap their minds on the present bandages
 the fruits of love are a cure only for leaving me behind in the wind of confrontation

I am the hospital
I do not have any patients
you are seeking a stethoscope
that is unmatched by the heavens
A barter of what I call my faith and love
Will, there ever be
a vacant space
in this love carriage
called the emergency room

My Heart Straps Across the Racetrack

With stirrups as heartbeats,
I loved to break through my low expectations
I wanted to own a horse farm,
but to ride a horse I needed my health to be on a better racetrack
Awaiting just a mere chance to unbuckle the shackles of life came with family
My dad, mom, and grandpa took me down to the racetrack
As I watched the races I looked forward to seeing the champion of that day
It was always a blessing
to pet the winning horses race after race, thanks to my family
Each pat and rub on a horse's mane gave me wonder
Their neighs became their own symphonic range of imagination
The horses liked kids and the apples were their barn of excitement
But those horses called Sickle Cell and Strength never responded well to my track
Always spitting out good apples, chewing the rotten ones, and never giving me a
place to race
Jockeying was a goal for me but with shame and hurt
I couldn't race with these horses
And yet with this discouragement, I still raced in my dreams
My blood made me the shape of a sickle but the shape of a jockey is my calling
And as I chronicled this, I felt that the horses I was jockeying in my dream
Still had a clean pasture for me to lie my head under the endless gazing sky
Neighing a chorus,
my heart in a gentle stirrup,
With my race beginning in the valleys of the night
along a laminating track showcased by twinkling oxygen-filled stars

Part 2: Dreams fulfilled

Another Sign Under

I am a Scorpio
Sensitive and intuitive
People outside our signs see us as sneaky
Being sneaky with our moods from day to dawn,
Piece to piece till the nonsense falls out

I am a Scorpio
We see everything
Big eyes that are dissecting the cosmos
In a plastic chair
Seeing good and evil in ourselves

I am a Scorpio
We seek the world within the brows and stern faces
And yet the world seeks our intuitive graces
Over the years that have identified the abusers, liars, drug abusers
One-time encounters that have changed the structures of family

I am a Scorpio
I see through your lies
I see the cautious lifestyle
enrobed in emotional wealth

I am a Scorpio
Our mouths are the damages rectified by silence
To build damaged buildings and to douse extinguished bridges
and we will bring out your fears as if they were blots of poison

I am a Scorpio
The sign is guided by stars
So if you cross me you get to see the cosmic clash of a universe
That collapses as if two constellations collided with one another

I Rest Well In The Lion's Den

The wealth of knowledge waits at the feet of those who are weary,
For those in need of love and joy,
And when all becomes too much, their pain
Becomes the splendor of the heart
But we need people to sit in the cage with us
Crossing the valleys of shame and the pride of mountaintops,
Not with picket fences but with vulnerable mesh windows
In times of strength, we must be the Daniel that lifts up the people
In trouble, a friend shouldn't be annoyed
Let's uphold the world and hold big fans in place instead of fangs
Me and you, right? We together could do many things!
And those who have a relationship with weary feet.
carrying of one's burden should be fulfilled
Preaching the den of lions to the lost and hungry
Setting up a vegan chorus for a den of experienced hunters
that desire love
The household of faith welcomes one another
Through the blood of Christ whose sandals break
To help anyone and everyone faithfully
To the cause of preaching joy to those sitting as lonely lions

Patient Wedding Bands

In a marriage there is patience
Clasped together like an exercise band
The considerate spouse is the holder
But the tension may stretch and bend the material
We feel the imperfection of the foundation
The missteps of life
The cracks of drama
The mistakes hobbled over the addition of new family members
And humanness is what comes from the shortcomings
We can't break the elasticity
We must grow close with tension
But the spousal support is with the perfection of us
The movement of a band
In an exercise band, drumming your fingers for work
Give God's grace a timetable not for yourself but for your own growth
It is your growth and the Lord is with you
The spousal support is the warm loving embrace
As you see that the cords begin to stretch
Just know that it is all coming back together as a rubber band ball
Straps of insecurities, heartbreaks, and turmoil
But we'll be all rolling together through the valleys and hills
From the "I do" to the "Don't I need you more",
Oh, what is a virtue called patience?

Give Voice

(Inspired by ONL Benjamin's poem "LET'S TALK" from his book Real Talk)

Give Voice to the seeds that are sprouting for tomorrow- Lest they turn into Weeds
Give Voice to the fallen - Give Voice to the renewal of the mind
Give Voice to the real talks that escalate into marriages and therapy sessions

Give Voice About How To Help One Further their friend's dreams without
  diminishing their own.
Give Voice to the past that doesn't need to be gifted with present mistakes
Give Voice to our Elder's decisions- - Give voice to the pains of healing trauma
Give Voice to the truth that our lies once hid- May we give voice to the solemn
oaths
  of trust

Give Voice to the families that raised you, spiritual and physical blood alike
Running through, chopping up statements, and holding air like a bike
As the wheels run rampant
with the shared knowledge of our distanced circumstances
Branch until
we meet the stances
That is political or biblical with the authorizing voices of those in need
Giving and partitioning
on the isles of a lovely voice
that associates with the roof that we raise
with the hands of champions
and empty tears into the glass of defeat

Give Voice to the living proof
That when our mental ability reaches stability to hold everything down
The only divide
Becomes our pride
Either we are lions giving voice
Or lying without any choice. Give voice.

5 Years Out of Sight

Fighting in my sleep while in glasses
A long time in the mirror
5 years without driving
And that is not the focus
As it was not what we could see
I was vain with my looks
I was pretending that I could see
5 years in the dark
Now in the light when I got those Costco premiums
I was finally able to see
My husband said "You goofy, are you crying"
And I was, with waterfalls cascading down my ebony skin
Embracing both the shadows and hues of the light in a breezy day
Eyeing the birds in the sky, seeing the trees whistle and swoon to me
Yet before all this, I was in the impending dark
blind to the Hawaii landscape around me
blind to the love that my family gave me for 5 years
Blind to the oceans that carried my dreams with a trancing glance
And when I saw those around me, I feel that angels have cleansed my eyes
A shield of protection and wisdom constructed into vocals of amusing sights
And now I see the blessings when I have them rest upon my eyes
I am blessed with the combat in the prescription glasses
Now instead of fighting off the darkness
I can embrace the light and warmth of my family here in Hawaii
Thank you, God, for through you I can see!

Don't Take Things Personally

Don't neglect the stores of wisdom I bring
That the truth is a neglectful being from a neglectful view
Creatures that are personal
Scorpios that are empathetic
we are the circus antics that increase the pandemonium
Of impersonal impacts that people take for jokes
And take for granted, behaviors
That we mask with shame
Or tell others to wear

Because it is better than wearing either a long mask or a temporary one
Highlighting In bright yellow ink "Not my problem"
Or writing our with dark Sharpie "Isn't my problem"
Essential items are not unwanted
But It is emotions
that cause me
to reset
and please
this view
Of people taking things personally

So Much Better

I feel
So much better
When I write on a planner
Again and Again
I am 60 and for 45 years I have kept this
All my scribbles
My eyes in the book of planned successes
My meditation
My hiding place is in scheduled work
15 minutes planned
45 years have passed
And there is consistency
With my meditation
And as I wake up
Early in the morning
On the rise of the reflection ourselves with the sun
With the goals that echo these thoughts
Well planned
And goal driven to the point of a happy life.

Dig

I give unto others
I dig into the graves of people's hearts
My own heart is a treasure trove
We have to dig
Into our hearts
And share more generously with
Our time
Our space
Our property
Our authority
Our money
And regardless of the bare ground we see
We are just moments away from hitting the diamond
Encrusted with the reward of charity and humanity.

For Better or For Worse

I blame my caretakers
My parents
Not rougher beginnings
Our faith in God can push
Through anything martial
For better or for worse is a blame game
We have a role in our works
We have to take responsibility
And lay that on a passage that sinks into our own souls
Our marriage to ourselves
To be the better person
In harmony
With bettering communities
That do not give thanks to the blame game we call
A hard knock life with an empty door walled off with rubber
Bouncing our pain away until it shatters rejected
And swiftly off the rocking chair of the marriage counselor's couch
Wondering to the therapist how much I blame my caretakers.

Today

Today is July 9th, Naomi's birthday
The first girl in a family of four boys
The nurses couldn't contain the news of a girl heralding the change of times
Nurses ran screaming about the arrival of a Humphrey girl
Grandmothers and grandfathers alike called from around their expanding world
Wondering what was this new Humphrey baby like
Naomi: Naomi Alzenia….Middle name after her maternal grandmother
Yet she was sent to care outside my own arms
The neonatal care as she
Was not breathing, details were covered up in scrubs
With her father also covered up in scrubs
Dressed just like a nurse but had the dedication of a neurosurgeon
Just wanting to make sure all was right
And through the commotion of reviving her, the nurses glanced at dad
Looked at his eyes and said "He's not Dr. Henderson, get him out of there"
Dad screamed "what is wrong with my baby", he couldn't leave with this barrier
The barrier of standing outside where they enforced the law
Peering at a baby in the unknown
Dad goes into the room
Tells of the bells and whistles attached to Naomi's small body
But said it will be all okay
But the storm of life that Dad told
Of her grand entrances, bloomed her life
Oh what a marvelous person as she makes the institutions reach for awards for her
School classes to be skipped and then humbled by her scholarship
The ticker parade after a national championship is a slight parade for her wit
As the scrubs that held her breathing are now college robes from UCLA
Front row on this day of July 9th, we see today as unlike any other day for Naomi

Camp Humphrey

Oh, I told my son to relay the news
Of the house that fostered 238 children over 15 years
With doors of gold
Hearts of valuable jewels
Faith like concrete
Windows that painted themselves
Floors of emerald
Babies in pampers
12 loads of laundry
A shopping list the size of a New York penthouse
Eggs more bountiful than a morning in the deep South
50 pancake making days that would bring tears to Paul Bunyan
Bunched with Oreos and Lays
Doors of love opened to the backs of these planted kisses
And smiles from the swings that held our home abode
Crawling kids like Army ROTC finishing drills for a paper diploma
Oh those were the days
That Camp Humphrey
Carried rotisserie chicken as an entree
With Ice Cream that called out Antarctica as if it was an ice cube versus freezers
And the beef hamburgers that would make a fortunate farmhand count their blessings
This was my Humphrey House
A camp for the kids starving for love
Wanting kisses and family care
Without a place to be planted kisses on their childish faces
A home that was never without love or a shortage of resources
Whenever one walked into the House, I want them to be a roller coasters
With smiles
And dips of incoming surprises
That leave a lifetime of memories
For when they depart the ride that is Camp Humphrey
I want them to return again to a home that is a revolving door of love.

My Baby

My baby was brought to me in the middle of the night
Golden hair, eyes like the sea. as a 10 month old
Trying to figure out what the world was
He fell right into the arms of dad
With a heart of strangeness seeing me
Dad was his hug person and slept the night with him
He loved to hold people, laughing, and was standoffish to me

But 3 weeks after his first visit
I took a nap and he walked in the room and got in the bed with me
And he tucked himself right under me
That was the spark that began to connect us like chicken and waffles
People stared at a black mom with a blonde baby
A drunk woke up and told me I won't say anything about you stealing the baby
But with all those stares and rude remarks, my golden hair baby will have a home

This baby rubbing and holding my face in his glowing white hands, was a map to a
  cocoon
That was wrapped within my own love and desire to protect him
With eyes more puzzled than a 1,000 piece jigsaw
A mind that loved the feeling of butterfly kisses
an eyelash on his cheek which made him want more
With the faint wisp of saying "Butterfly, Butterfly"

My Baby was brought in the middle of the night
A baby to many but a precious gift to me from the Lord above
6 years younger than most in the house, 29 years away from the eldest
And it felt like the world was alive in this

Storytelling with Pringles

When they first brought Jeremy to the house
I didn't see him in the first 45 minutes
Naomi hugged him and got him so close
He was held with so much time and space,
Naomi was 6 years old and grabbed Jeremy, 3 years old in her arms
A little brother just appeared in the night
Jeremy was shy, big hair and spoke more spanish than english
When dad took him out, Jeremy wanted snacks
Looking at dad
Making curves on his lips with fingertips
But then in the store he painted his own imagination
The pringles can has a mustache
With what he gave dad was joy in his own painting of life
One night I heard him speaking in spanish and I was wondering
What could this boy of storytelling hands and astounding vision be saying
I had a Cuban neighbor help me translate
They said he was praying for the family with the brown faces
The man with the good family
A sister, who was little crazy, but they liked her
Dressed her up, does her hair
So God please let them stay here and be in this cookie smelling house
With lots of food and snacks
With the quiet names with the vision
His listening with the art of a paint brush stroke
And it was so that when we hug him close
We see the art that has dazzled so many
But for them it is the love he brings into our humble abode
Royal, unforgettable, Jeremiah

Eyes of a Smiling Child

Josiah with the marks of the tales of 7-month-olds
With no sight and ability to walk
Needless to say he needed glasses
So he didn't see the world like I did
His troubled legs
He crawled everywhere
Skinny and clammy
But he was trying to push forward
Scrawny and super sweet
Like a sweaty yellow Minion but he was a love
We wanted so much to hold him
And build from the ear surgeries, eye surgeries
Twice in a row, glasses
Allergies, so sweet
With walking he had no depth perception
And it looked like he had to lift above mountains
Swings, escalators, and different rides were monsters in his gaze
But his first really good glasses were great
And he smiled seeing me for the first time
He started crying and smiling
He looked at all of us and was overwhelmed with so many views
He saw Amazing Jakes and was in love with it all
His talent is in the cartoon figures
A job at Disney at the age of 10 and he made his product developer
Leading projects that his ideas arose
With his shows even gracing the Disney Channel
Yet Josiah wore the world in his glasses
And he made sure that the distance between him and the stars were never far apart
When he created digital figures he made stars
With his vision he directed the course of the time of those around him
So yes a world changer is what I see
But each and every day, I hope he sees how much he means to me as my baby
The one who smiled when he placed those thick glasses onto his eyes
And finally saw the family
he dreamed about
without having
to close his eyes.
Josiah, don't close your imaginative eyes ever again.

Word of Mouth

She was taller
Big face
Curly hair
Giant eyes
Crocodile Tears
Great performances
Protector of her twin
Takes the share
Of protecting as a Giant with a beanstalk
Coupled with the mouth of a sailor
Opinionated, stand-up, cocky, with the world ahead
Protesting the immigration laws against Latinos
Wanting to rattle against the officials
Understanding the political and Latino community
She is a beauty model
Makeup
The 2nd girl of 9 kids
Fleshed with the patience of the world
But she grants demands as if they were court orders
Her wild imaginations
Her art and style
It is unmatched
By no one
Not those of who she wards away
But the family that guards her
And I hope one day
She takes that Jack
Throw that nuisance off her floating house
And waits until the sunrise to
come off her high pedestal of a home
To truly open up and receive the love around her

Blended Families

Out of respect and privacy we won't reveal pictures but their bond will be written in poetry

I thought about one more poem
Combining what was to be one more family
One more word on how we became blended
From 2 sides of a road
2 different locations to New York
Mt Vernon to Queens
And Delaware being the connector
I didn't want to leave my new family unconnected
Name my story a bond, that those two boys formed
Dad and I first introduced them in a park
We pretended that we didn't know each other
Mirrored the words that we saw every Saturday for a few weeks
Sitting across from another view, with seats never near the first time
Overtime the boys became friends
Bonded over the lunches and the Happy Meals that
bridged a bond never broken
The boys were 7 and 9 whisperings that me and Dad should date
Laughing at this as if it was their own plan
We followed the brave boys and their concoction of a plan
Which we already wrote the ingredients to
And when the boys are the only children of their other parents.
Together we became whole,
coming together with us as we had kids was fun for them.
Both of them lived with their other parent
and came to us on weekends.
They both went off to college
one at a time
and went on with their lives.
Both are older adults now.
And how I would word it, with all the strategic planning done
I couldn't help but to laugh that this was a poem that started this very book

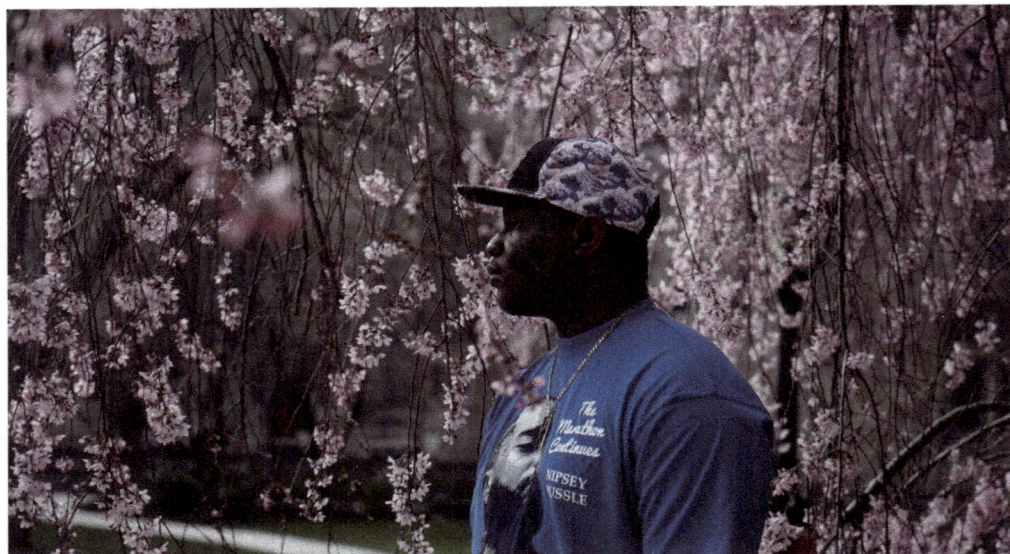

About The Author

Noah Humphrey (Knowa Know) is the author of Morgan: Memoir of South Central LA; a published poet; and a trailblazer. Born in Wilmington Delaware, Noah's parents stayed in multiple places but Noah's pivotal moment was as a teen in South Central LA. South Central was a place where Noah started tenaciously writing poems, preaching, and developing a huge passion for football. By the time he was 21, he became the spiritual advisor/chaplain of the Whittier College Football team; Earned his B.A. in Religious Studies with a minor in Holistic Care; inducted in Theta Alpha Kappa, religious studies Honor Society; and became a mighty proud Orthogonian, emulating leadership which he would call for civil justice and peace. Noah will be graduating in May 2023 with a Master of Divinity degree from Yale Divinity School. He has a volunteer role with Athletes in Action(AIA) serving in a chaplaincy role for the Yale Football Team since the Fall of 2021. He assisted Team 149, the 2022 Yale Football Team, to its first outright Ivy League Championship since 2017. After a gap year, Noah will be attending the Southern California University of Health Sciences to pursue a Ph.D. in Chiropractic Medicine. He also seeks to do outreach ministry, football coaching, and counseling. As a current settler of the sovereign nation of Hawai'i on the island of O'ahu, he seeks to be the change he wants to see in the world.

About The Author

Meryl Victoria Humphrey was born Meryl V. Henry in Jamaica Estates Hospital in Queens, New York. Meryl, who was affectionately called "Woody" as a child, lived a life in which she was exposed to people from all walks of life at a very early age. Her parents George and Alzenia say she became a "Student that analyzed people" extremely early in life. Her observations caused her to see and understand things well beyond her years. Born with Sickle Cell Thalassemia her parents nor her brother Darryl allowed her or anyone else to limit her dreams. She was told and encouraged to do anything that anyone else could do. When others were scared for her and said "No" she pushed forward and said "Yes, I can". So thus began the journey of defiance and determination to prove them wrong. Little Woody would dance barefoot in the rain in a beautiful dress while watering the grass. She was and still is …. A Dreamer.

Book Dedication from Meryl Humphrey

I would like to dedicate this book to Dettra Woodard and Sherene Gulley, my two "book end" friends that loved me and held me down during my time in Fresno, CA, and once I moved to Los Angeles. I've had many Warrior Friends that came and left us to live out their eternal life in Heaven BUT these two were special. They were cheerleaders, spirit builders, and comedians who nourished my body and soul. I miss them and think about them often. I continue to run this race and every so often I slow down and can see them waving crimson colored flags from the stands, cheering me on.

Sometimes, we go through the worst moments of sickle cell disorder,
Sometimes, we experience the most horrific type of sickle cell crisis,
Sometimes, we encounter the most horrible form of sickle cell complications,
At other times, we suffer the most shameful moment of sickle cell stigma,
And at other times, we are victims of the most terrible form of sickle cell abuse.
But after it all,
We do not look like what we have been through,
Simply because the Grace of God has kept us,
And the same Grace of God will continue to sustain us.
As sickle cell warriors,
we are built to survive.

Dedication page from the heart of Meryl
Artistic credit: Elisabeth Humphrey

Shantee Sayles

Released from Heaven: 3/26/93   Returned to Heaven: 05/09/17

Angela Barlow

Released from Heaven: 8/21/93   Returned to Heaven: 10/27/16

www.ingramcontent.com/pod-product-compliance
Lightning Source LLC
Chambersburg PA
CBHW051713090426
42736CB00013B/2687